EASY HUNGARIAN COOKBOOK

AUTHENTIC HUNGARIAN COOKING

By
Chef Maggie Chow
Copyright © 2015 by Saxonberg Associates

Published by
BookSumo, a division of Saxonberg Associates
http://www.booksumo.com/

INTRODUCTION

Welcome to *The Effortless Chef Series*! Thank you for taking the time to download the *Easy Hungarian Cookbook*. Come take a journey with me into the delights of easy cooking. The point of this cookbook and all my cookbooks is to exemplify the effortless nature of cooking simply.

In this book we focus on Hungarian. You will find that even though the recipes are simple, the taste of the dishes is quite amazing.

So will you join me in an adventure of simple cooking? If the answer is yes (and I hope it is) please consult the table of contents to find the dishes you are most interested in. Once you are ready jump right in and start cooking.

— Chef Maggie Chow

TABLE OF CONTENTS

Introduction 2

Table of Contents 3

Any Issues? Contact Me 7

Legal Notes 8

Common Abbreviations 9

Chapter 1: Easy Hungarian Recipes 10

   Hungarian Poppy Seed Pastry 10

   Classical Pretzels 13

   Red Cabbage and Thighs 16

   Pork Soup 19

   Bittersweet Sweet Eastern European Crepes 22

   Classical Torte 25

   The Best Fatback Brisket 28

   Pickled Florets 31

Cream of Noodle 34

Paprika Stew from Hungary 37

Paprika Mushroom and Parsley Stew 40

Hungarian Dessert I 43

Eastern European Sherry Pork Chops 46

Hungarian Cabbage 48

Hungarian Egg Noodles 50

Bread from Eastern Europe 52

Hungarian Sour Cream Bake 55

Hungarian Mashed Liver 57

Bacon Potatoes and Chicken 60

Hungarian Cream Cheese Cookies 63

Vegetable Hungarian Stew 66

Potato and Coconut Dessert 69

Maggie's Favorite Goulash 71

Honey Dessert 73

Easy Hungarian Goulash 76

Beef and Pepper Bake 78

Sausage and Pepper Bake 80

Hungarian Stew 82

Hungarian Bread Spice 84

Mustard and Paprika Chicken 86

Hungarian Chicken 88

Vinegar Salad 91

Paprika Fish 93

Czech Pancakes 95

All Pork and Sausage Stew 97

Hungary Pepper Salsa 99

Hungarian Dump Dinner 101

Dumplings from Hungary 104

Eastern European Breakfast 106

Rustic Roast 108

Tomato Ribs 111

Hungarian Topping for Bread 113

Potatoes from Eastern Europe 115

Mushrooms and Sour Cream Stew 117

Classical Hungarian Stew (Lecsó) 119

Pork with Creamy Mushrooms (Jagerschnitzel) 121

Dumplings in Germany I (Spaetzle) 124

Dumplings in Germany II (Semmelknoedel) 126

Cabbage and Apples 129

Beef Rolls of Bacon, Onions, and Pickles (Rouladen) 131

Eastern European Meat Pastries 133

THANKS FOR READING! NOW LET'S TRY SOME **SUSHI** AND **DUMP DINNERS** 135

Come On 137

Let's Be Friends :) 137

Can I Ask A Favour? 138

Interested in Other Easy Cookbooks? 139

ANY ISSUES? CONTACT ME

If you find that something important to you is missing from this book please contact me at maggie@booksumo.com.

I will try my best to re-publish a revised copy taking your feedback into consideration and let you know when the book has been revised with you in mind.

:)

— Chef Maggie Chow

Legal Notes

Common Abbreviations

cup(s)	C.
tablespoon	tbsp
teaspoon	tsp
ounce	oz.
pound	lb

*All units used are standard American measurements

Chapter 1: Easy Hungarian Recipes

Hungarian Poppy Seed Pastry

Ingredients

- 5 tbsps white sugar
- 1 C. unsalted butter, cubed
- 3 egg yolks
- 1 (8 oz.) container sour cream
- 4 C. self-rising flour
- 1 (.25 oz.) package active dry yeast

Filling:

- 1 C. whole milk
- 1 C. white sugar
- 2 1/2 C. finely diced walnuts
- 1 lemon, zested
- 2/3 C. golden raisins
- 1 egg
- 1 tbsp water

Directions

- Get a jellyroll pan and cover it with parchment paper before doing anything else.
- Add a dough blade to your food processor and process the following to form a dough: sour cream, flour, 5 tbsps sugar, yeast, egg yolks, and butter.

- Now form the dough into a ball and place it in a bowl with a damp kitchen towel over the bowl.
- Begin to heat 1 C. of sugar and milk while stirring until the sugar is fully incorporated into the mix.
- Continue heating everything until the mix thickens. Then combine in the walnuts, shut the heat, and add the raisins and lemon zest.
- Break your dough into 3 pieces then shape one piece into a rectangle on a cutting board coated with flour. Leave the rest of the dough in the bowl.
- Layer 1/3 of the walnut mix over the rectangle with some space on the edges.
- Now roll the dough into a cylinder and crimp the seam to seal everything.
- Place the cylinder on the jellyroll pan. Then continue doing the same thing with the rest of the dough.
- Get a small bowl and mix a tbsp of water with the egg and whisk it together.
- Coat your rolled dough with the mix then leave everything for 60 mins.
- Top the dough again with the egg mix then place the entire jellyroll pan in the fridge for 40 mins.
- Set your oven to 375 degrees before doing anything else.
- Once the oven is hot cook everything in the oven for 40 mins.
- Enjoy.

Amount per serving (24 total)

Timing Information:

Preparation	30 m
Cooking	35 m
Total Time	2 h 35 m

Nutritional Information:

Calories	314 kcal
Fat	18.9 g
Carbohydrates	32.8g
Protein	5.5 g
Cholesterol	58 mg
Sodium	279 mg

* Percent Daily Values are based on a 2,000 calorie diet.

CLASSICAL PRETZELS

Ingredients

- 2 C. flour
- 1/2 C. butter
- 3/4 C. milk
- 1 1/2 tsps yeast
- 3 tsps sugar
- 3 tsps salt, divided
- 1 tsp water
- 1 egg yolk
- 1 tsp flour
- 1 tsp hot water

Directions

- Get your milk hot in a pan then add it to a bowl, with the sugar and yeast.
- Stir the mix until the sugar is fully incorporated then let the mix stand for 15 mins.
- At the same time get a 2nd bowl and mix: 1 tsp butter, 1 tsp salt, and the flour.
- Add yeast and stir the mix.
- Keep working everything until you have a ball then break the dough into 4 pieces.
- Form each piece into a ball again and place everything in a bowl.
- Place a kitchen towel around the bowl and let everything sit for 45 mins.

- Now set your oven to 375 degrees before doing anything else.
- Take one piece of dough and break it into four more pieces.
- Roll each piece of dough into a long rope and shape it into a pretzel.
- Lay all the pretzels on a cookie sheet and continue forming pretzels in the same manner.
- Now get a small bowl and mix 1 tsp with your egg. Coat your pretzels with the egg wash then cook everything in the oven for 13 mins.
- At the same time get a 2nd small bowl and combine: 2 tsp hot water, 1 tsp flour, 2 tsp salt. Stir the mix until it is thick then top the pretzels with the salt mix and cook them for 4 more mins in the oven.
- Enjoy.

Amount per serving: 1

Timing Information:

Preparation	10 m
Total Time	1 h 20 m

Nutritional Information:

Calories	122.8
Fat	6.6g
Cholesterol	28.6mg
Sodium	483.4mg
Carbohydrates	13.5g
Protein	2.3g

* Percent Daily Values are based on a 2,000 calorie diet.

Red Cabbage and Thighs

Ingredients

- 4 slices bacon, optional
- 1 tbsp bacon drippings
- 1/4 C. all-purpose flour
- 1/2 tsp kosher salt
- 1/2 tsp smoked paprika
- 2 lbs skinless chicken thighs
- 1 red onion, sliced
- 1 large apple, cored and sliced
- 1 head red cabbage, cored and sliced
- 1/2 C. red wine vinegar
- 1/4 C. dry red wine
- 1/4 C. brown sugar
- 1/2 tsp ground cinnamon (optional)

Directions

- Set your oven to 350 degrees before doing anything else.
- Fry your bacon until it is fully done, for about 12 mins, then remove them from the pan and break everything into pieces.
- Get a bowl, combine: paprika, kosher salt, and flour.
- Top your pieces of chicken with this mix then sear the chicken all over in the bacon drippings for 6 mins each side.
- Now remove the meat from the pan.

- Remove most of the bacon drippings but keep about 2 tbsps and begin to stir fry your apple and onions in it for 7 mins then combine in the bacon, and red cabbage.
- Top everything with some more salt and stir the mix for 7 more mins.
- Now add in your red vinegar.
- Stir the mix then add in the cinnamon and brown sugar.
- Stir the mix again and get everything boiling.
- Once the mix is boiling, lower the heat, and let everything cook for 12 mins until half of the liquid evaporates.
- Stir the mix as it cooks.
- Now place your chicken on top the cabbage and put everything in the oven for 45 mins.
- Enjoy.

Amount per serving (8 total)

Timing Information:

Preparation	20 m
Cooking	1 h 10 m
Total Time	1 h 30 m

Nutritional Information:

Calories	287 kcal
Fat	11 g
Carbohydrates	23.9g
Protein	22.5 g
Cholesterol	74 mg
Sodium	295 mg

* Percent Daily Values are based on a 2,000 calorie diet.

PORK SOUP

Ingredients

- 5 slices bacon, diced
- 2 large onions, diced
- 1/4 C. Hungarian paprika
- 1 1/2 tsps garlic powder
- 1/4 tsp ground black pepper
- 5 lbs boneless pork chops, trimmed
- 1 large yellow bell pepper, seeded and diced
- 2 (14 oz.) cans diced tomatoes, with liquid
- 2/3 C. beef broth
- 2 C. reduced-fat sour cream
- 2 (6 oz.) packages wide egg noodles

Directions

- Cook your bacon for 12 mins then drain the oils into a small bowl for later.
- Add the onions to the pot and fry them until they are see-through.
- Shut the heat and add in: the pepper, garlic powder, and paprika. Then pour everything into a saucepan.
- Add some of the bacon grease to the skillet again and fry your pork until it is browned all over and fully done. Cook the pork in batches and add in more drippings after each batch.

- Once all the pork has been cooked place them to the side on a cutting board and dice the pork into small pieces. Then add the meat into the saucepan.
- Add a bit more bacon grease to the skillet and begin to stir fry your bell peppers until they are tender then add this to the saucepan as well.
- Pour in the broth and tomatoes with juice into the saucepan then get everything boiling.
- Once the mix is boiling, set the heat to low, and let everything gently boil for 1.5 hrs. Now add the sour cream, stir the mix, and shut the heat.
- Now boil your noodles in water and salt for 7 mins. Remove the liquid and divide the noodles between serving bowls.
- Top each bowl with the tomato mix and serve.
- Enjoy.

Amount per serving (14 total)

Timing Information:

Preparation	20 m
Cooking	1 h 55 m
Total Time	2 h 15 m

Nutritional Information:

Calories	323 kcal
Fat	13.2 g
Carbohydrates	22.9g
Protein	26.9 g
Cholesterol	86 mg
Sodium	349 mg

* Percent Daily Values are based on a 2,000 calorie diet.

BITTERSWEET SWEET EASTERN EUROPEAN CREPES

Ingredients

- 2 C. all-purpose flour
- 2 eggs
- 1 C. milk
- 1 C. soda water
- 1/2 C. vegetable oil
- 1 pinch salt

Almond Filling:

- 1 C. diced almonds
- 1/2 C. white sugar

- 1/4 C. milk
- 1/4 tsp vanilla extract
- 1 1/2 tsps rum (optional)

Chocolate Topping:

- 1/4 C. water
- 1/2 C. white sugar
- 1/2 C. diced bittersweet chocolate
- 2 tbsps margarine

Directions

- Get a bowl, mix: eggs and flour.
- Once the mix is smooth combine in: salt, milk, veggie oil, and carbonated water.

- Stir the mix until it is smooth then place a covering on the bowl and put everything in the fridge for 8 hrs.
- Now coat a skillet with nonstick spray then stir your batter.
- Once the skillet is hot ladle 1/4 C. of batter into it and fry the mix for 60 secs then flip it and fry everything for 60 more secs.
- Place the pancake on some wax paper and continue making pancakes in this manner.
- Once all of the pancakes are done begin heat and stir the following: rum, almonds, vanilla, 1/2 C. sugar, and milk.
- Heat the mix with a low level of heat then stir everything until it is thick. Now shut the heat.
- Now get a separate pot and begin to heat and stir the following as well: 1/2 C. sugar, water, and chocolate.
- Heat the mix with a low level of heat until everything is smooth.
- Shut the heat and stir in the margarine until everything is smooth.
- Coat 1 pancake with a large tbsp of almond mix then roll the pancake and put it in a casserole dish.
- Continue topping and rolling all the pancakes in this manner.
- Coat everything with your chocolate sauce.
- Enjoy.

Amount per serving (5 total)

Timing Information:

Preparation	40 m
Cooking	30 m
Total Time	9 h 10 m

Nutritional Information:

Calories	873 kcal
Fat	47.4 g
Carbohydrates	98.7g
Protein	15.1 g
Cholesterol	71 mg
Sodium	104 mg

* Percent Daily Values are based on a 2,000 calorie diet.

CLASSICAL TORTE

Ingredients

- 2 C. diced walnuts
- 1 tsp ground cinnamon
- 3/4 C. white sugar
- 1/4 C. warm water (110 degrees F/45 degrees C)
- 1 (.25 oz.) envelope active dry yeast
- 1 tsp white sugar
- 4 egg yolks
- 1/2 C. sour cream
- 1 1/3 C. butter or margarine, softened
- 4 1/2 C. all-purpose flour
- 1 (16 oz.) jar apricot preserves
- 4 egg whites
- 2/3 C. white sugar

Directions

- Coat a jellyroll pan with oil then set your oven to 350 degrees before doing anything else.
- Get a bowl, combine: 3/4 C. sugar, walnuts, and ground cinnamon.
- Get a 2nd bowl and mix 1 tsp of sugar, yeast, and some warm water.
- Leave this mix to sit for 15 mins.
- Get a 3rd bowl, combine: butter, yeast mix: sour cream, and egg yolks.

- Stir the mix until it is smooth then add the flour slowly until you have a slightly stiff dough.
- Work the dough with your hands for 7 mins. Then break the dough into three pieces then shape each piece into a ball.
- Place the balls on a cutting board coated with flour and place a damp kitchen towel over them. Let the balls sit for 20 mins.
- Roll out one piece of dough to the same size as your jellyroll pan. Then lay the dough in the pan and top it with 3/4 of the nut mix.
- Do the same thing for another piece of dough then place it in the pan as well. Top it with the apricot and add the last piece of the dough in the same manner over everything.
- Cook the layers in the oven for 45 mins.
- Begin to whisk your egg whites until peaking then slowly mix in 2/3 of a C. of sugar into the eggs.
- Top the layers with this mix then layer the rest of your nuts on top of everything.
- Continue cooking the contents in the oven for 17 more mins.
- Let the mix sit for a bit then serve.
- Enjoy.

Amount per serving (32 total)

Timing Information:

Preparation	20 m
Cooking	1 h 10 m
Total Time	1 h 30 m

Nutritional Information:

Calories	267 kcal
Fat	14.1 g
Carbohydrates	32.8g
Protein	4.1 g
Cholesterol	48 mg
Sodium	71 mg

* Percent Daily Values are based on a 2,000 calorie diet.

The Best Fatback Brisket

Ingredients

- 5 lbs beef brisket
- 2 lbs sliced bacon
- 5 C. brewed coffee
- 1/4 C. salt
- 1 C. butter
- 1/2 C. minced garlic
- 1/2 C. shortening
- 1 lb fatback, sliced into small rectangles
- 2 sweet potatoes, quartered
- 1 C. olive oil
- 2 1/2 tbsps prepared horseradish

Directions

- Cover your brisket with bacon then place everything into a casserole dish.
- Combine your salt and coffee and top the brisket with this mix.
- Place a covering of foil over the dish and let the brisket sit in the fridge for 8 hrs.
- Begin to stir and heat your garlic and butter until the butter has turned to a golden color.
- Coat a roasting pan with the shortening and place your brisket in it.

- Top the brisket with 1 C. of coffee mix and place your fatback over the brisket.
- Layer your potatoes around the brisket and top everything with the butter mix.
- Place a lid or some foil on the pan and let it sit for 60 mins.
- Now set your oven to 325 degrees before doing anything else.
- Cook the brisket in the oven, once it is hot, for 4 hrs.
- Once the brisket is done begin to heat and occasionally stir your olive oil and horseradish with a low level of heat for 30 mins then enjoy everything as a dipping sauce with the brisket after you have carved it into pieces.
- Enjoy.

Amount per serving (20 total)

Timing Information:

Preparation	1 h
Cooking	4 h
Total Time	13 h

Nutritional Information:

Calories	802 kcal
Fat	78.6 g
Carbohydrates	14.3g
Protein	19.1 g
Cholesterol	121 mg
Sodium	2172 mg

* Percent Daily Values are based on a 2,000 calorie diet.

PICKLED FLORETS

Ingredients

- 4 C. distilled white vinegar
- 4 C. water
- 1/2 C. sea salt
- 1 head cauliflower, broken into florets
- 3 hot chile peppers, sliced lengthwise
- 3 cloves garlic, minced, divided
- 1 tbsp mustard seed, divided
- 1 tbsp whole black peppercorns, divided
- 1 tbsp coriander seeds, divided
- 1 tbsp dill seeds, divided
- 1 tbsp allspice berries, divided
- 1 1/2 tsps red pepper flakes, divided
- 3 bay leaves
- 3 1-quart canning jars with lids and rings, lids and jars sterilized in boiling water for 10 mins

Directions

- Get the following simmering: salt, water, and vinegar.
- Now fill each jar with: 1 bay leaf, 1/3 cauliflower, 1/2 tsp pepper flakes, 1 hot pepper, 1 tsp berries, 1 mince piece of garlic, 1 tsp dill, 1 tsp mustard seed, 1 tsp coriander seed, and 1 tsp peppercorns.

- Divide the vinegar mix between the jars and leave half an inch of space in each jar.
- With a knife break any bubbles of air in each jar by running the knife along the sides slowly. Then clean the top of the jar and place the lids and rings on them.
- Add a rack to a large pot then add in enough water to fill the pot halfway. Get the water boiling then place the jars in the water with some tongs.
- The jars should be submerged in the water with an additional inch of water over them.
- Get the water boiling again then place a lid on the pot, and let everything cook for 12 mins.
- Take out the jars, let them cool, and then store everything in an area without sunlight.
- Enjoy.

Amount per serving (39 total)

Timing Information:

Preparation	20 m
Cooking	10 m
Total Time	30 m

Nutritional Information:

Calories	9 kcal
Fat	< 0.2 g
Carbohydrates	< 1.7g
Protein	< 0.5 g
Cholesterol	0 mg
Sodium	1089 mg

* Percent Daily Values are based on a 2,000 calorie diet.

CREAM OF NOODLE

Ingredients

- 1 (16 oz.) package wide egg noodles
- 3 cubes chicken bouillon
- 1/4 C. water
- 1 (10.75 oz.) can condensed cream of mushroom soup
- 1/2 C. diced onion
- 2 tbsps Worcestershire sauce
- 1 tbsp poppy seeds
- 1/4 tsp garlic powder
- 1/4 tsp hot pepper sauce
- 2 C. cottage cheese
- 2 C. sour cream
- 1/4 C. grated Parmesan cheese
- 1 pinch paprika

Directions

- Get your noodles boiling in water and salt for 6 mins then remove all the liquids.
- Get a bowl and stir your bouillon cubes with some boiling water until it is smooth.
- Add in: hot sauce, mushroom soup, garlic powder, diced onion, poppy seeds, and Worcestershire.
- Stir the mix again until it is smooth then add in: egg noodles, cottage cheese, and sour cream.

- Place everything into the crock of a slow cooker and top everything with some paprika and parmesan.
- Place the lid on the slow cooker and cook everything for 4 hrs with a high level of heat.
- Enjoy.

Amount per serving (10 total)

Timing Information:

Preparation	10 m
Cooking	5 h 10 m
Total Time	5 h 20 m

Nutritional Information:

Calories	365 kcal
Fat	16.5 g
Carbohydrates	39.3g
Protein	15.2 g
Cholesterol	67 mg
Sodium	826 mg

* Percent Daily Values are based on a 2,000 calorie diet.

Paprika Stew from Hungary

Ingredients

- 2 tbsps bacon grease
- 1 large onion, diced
- 3 cloves garlic, diced
- 3/4 tsp salt
- 1 tsp crushed red pepper flakes
- 3 tbsps paprika
- 1 (2 to 3 lb) whole chicken, cut into pieces
- 1 C. water
- 1 (14.5 oz.) can diced tomatoes
- 2 tbsps all-purpose flour
- 1 (8 oz.) container sour cream

Directions

- Begin frying the following in the bacon drippings: pepper flakes, onion, paprika, garlic, and salt.
- Fry the mix until the onions are see-through then combine in your chicken and submerge everything in water.
- Let the mix cook for 65 mins.

- Now add in the tomatoes and save the juice in a bowl.
- Add your sour cream and flour to the tomato juice and stir the mix until it is smooth.
- Pour the mix into the chicken and stir everything.
- Let the contents simmer until everything is thick.
- Enjoy.

Amount per serving (4 total)

Timing Information:

Preparation	15 m
Cooking	1 h 15 m
Total Time	1 h 30 m

Nutritional Information:

Calories	604 kcal
Fat	39.8 g
Carbohydrates	16g
Protein	43.9 g
Cholesterol	156 mg
Sodium	747 mg

* Percent Daily Values are based on a 2,000 calorie diet.

Paprika Mushroom and Parsley Stew

Ingredients

- 4 tbsps unsalted butter
- 2 C. diced onions
- 1 lb fresh mushrooms, sliced
- 2 tsps dried dill weed
- 1 tbsp paprika
- 1 tbsp soy sauce
- 2 C. chicken broth
- 1 C. milk
- 3 tbsps all-purpose flour
- 1 tsp salt
- ground black pepper to taste
- 2 tsps lemon juice
- 1/4 C. diced fresh parsley
- 1/2 C. sour cream

Directions

- Fry your onions in butter for 7 mins then combine in the mushrooms and continue frying them for 7 more mins.
- Now add the broth, dill, soy sauce, and paprika.
- Stir the mix and set the heat to low.
- Place a lid on the pot and let the contents gently boil for 17 mins.
- Get a bowl, combine the flour and milk until everything is smooth then add this mix to the simmering mix.
- Stir the flour mix then place the lid back on the pot and continue cooking everything for 17 more mins.

- Stir the mix a few more times as it simmers.
- Now stir in the sour cream, salt, parsley, black pepper, and lemon juice.
- Simmer the mix for 4 more mins.
- Enjoy.

Amount per serving (6 total)

Timing Information:

Preparation	15 m
Cooking	35 m
Total Time	50 m

Nutritional Information:

Calories	201 kcal
Fat	13.5 g
Carbohydrates	14.8g
Protein	7.5 g
Cholesterol	32 mg
Sodium	829 mg

* Percent Daily Values are based on a 2,000 calorie diet.

Hungarian Dessert I

Ingredients

- 12 oz. hazelnuts
- 2 tsps baking powder
- 6 egg yolks
- 5/8 C. white sugar
- 6 egg whites
- 1 pint heavy whipping cream
- 1/8 C. diced hazelnuts, for garnish

Directions

- Coat a spring form pan with oil and flour then set your oven to 325 degrees before doing anything else.
- Grind your hazelnuts and combine them with the baking powder in a bowl.
- Get a 2nd bowl and whisk your egg yolks with the sugar until it is pale.
- Stir the ground hazelnut mix and continue mixing everything until it is smooth.

- Get a separate whisk and in a 3rd bowl beat the egg whites until stiff then add a third of the eggs into the yolk mix. Add the rest of the eggs and make sure there are no streaks and everything is evenly combined.
- Enter the mix into your prepared pan and cook everything in the oven for 70 mins.
- Cut the cake into 3 pieces lengthwise and begin to beat the cream until it is stiff then top the cake with it.
- Garnish everything with some hazelnuts.
- Enjoy.

Amount per serving (12 total)

Timing Information:

Preparation	30 m
Cooking	1 h
Total Time	1 h 30 m

Nutritional Information:

Calories	399 kcal
Fat	35 g
Carbohydrates	17.1g
Protein	8.4 g
Cholesterol	157 mg
Sodium	128 mg

* Percent Daily Values are based on a 2,000 calorie diet.

Eastern European Sherry Pork Chops

Ingredients

- 4 pork chops
- salt and pepper to taste
- 1/4 C. all-purpose flour
- 1 C. sour cream
- 1/4 C. dry sherry
- 1/4 C. ketchup
- 1 tsp Worcestershire sauce
- 1/4 tsp paprika
- 1 bay leaf

Directions

- Coat your pieces of pork with pepper and salt. Then brown them in oil until they are fully done.
- Now remove any excess drippings from the pan.
- Get a bowl, combine: bay leaf, sour cream, paprika, sherry, Worcestershire, and ketchup.
- Stir the mix until it is smooth then combine it with the pork.
- Place a lid on the pan and let the mix gently boil with a low level of heat for 60 mins.
- Enjoy.

Amount per serving (3 total)

Timing Information:

Preparation	10 m
Cooking	1 h
Total Time	1 h 10 m

Nutritional Information:

Calories	376 kcal
Fat	24.5 g
Carbohydrates	19.9g
Protein	17.7 g
Cholesterol	79 mg
Sodium	430 mg

* Percent Daily Values are based on a 2,000 calorie diet.

Hungarian Cabbage

Ingredients

- 1 (16 oz.) package egg noodles
- 1/2 C. butter
- 1 large onion, diced
- 1 head cabbage, cored and diced
- salt and ground black pepper to taste

Directions

- Boil your noodles in water and salt for 6 mins then remove the liquids.
- Now begin to stir fry your onions in butter for 10 mins then add the cabbage and continue cooking the mix for 10 more mins.
- Add the noodles to the mix and top everything with some black pepper and salt.
- Enjoy.

Amount per serving (6 total)

Timing Information:

Preparation	15 m
Cooking	10 m
Total Time	25 m

Nutritional Information:

Calories	482 kcal
Fat	18.9 g
Carbohydrates	67g
Protein	13.5 g
Cholesterol	103 mg
Sodium	226 mg

* Percent Daily Values are based on a 2,000 calorie diet.

Hungarian Egg Noodles

Ingredients

- 1 (16 oz.) package egg noodles
- 3 1/2 slices smoked bacon
- 2 C. sour cream
- 1 (12 oz.) container cottage cheese
- salt to taste

Directions

- Set your oven to 350 degrees before doing anything else.
- Get your pasta boiling in water and salt for 9 mins then remove all the liquids.
- Begin to fry your bacon then break it into pieces and place it all to the side.
- Add the noodles to a casserole dish and top them with the sour cream, cottage cheese, and bacon.
- Add some salt as well then cook everything in the oven for 4 mins.
- Enjoy.

Amount per serving (8 total)

Timing Information:

Preparation	10 m
Cooking	15 m
Total Time	25 m

Nutritional Information:

Calories	438 kcal
Fat	22 g
Carbohydrates	43.6g
Protein	16.5 g
Cholesterol	87 mg
Sodium	365 mg

* Percent Daily Values are based on a 2,000 calorie diet.

BREAD FROM EASTERN EUROPE

Ingredients

- 1 (.25 oz.) package active dry yeast
- 1 3/4 C. warm milk
- 1 egg yolk
- 2 eggs
- 2 tbsps white sugar
- 2 tsps salt
- 5 C. all-purpose flour
- 1 tbsp poppy seeds
- 1 egg, beaten

Directions

- Get a bowl, combine your warm milk and yeast. Let the mix sit for 20 mins.
- Get a 2nd bowl, mix: salt, eggs, sugar, and egg yolks.
- Add in the yeast mix and also 3 C. of flour.
- Stir the mix evenly then add in the rest of the flour slowly.
- Form a dough from the mix then knead it for 10 mins on a floured working surface.
- Divide the dough into 2 pieces and shape everything into loaves.
- Let the loaves sit for 30 mins then divide each one in half. Shape each piece into a long rope.
- Braid the 4 pieces of dough and place everything on to a baking sheet.

- Place a damp kitchen towel over everything and let the dough rise for 50 mins.
- Now set your oven to 400 degrees before doing anything else.
- Top the dough with some whisked eggs and poppy seeds then cook everything in the oven for 20 mins.
- Now set the heat to 350 degrees and continue baking everything 40 more mins.
- Enjoy.

Amount per serving (12 total)

Timing Information:

Preparation	30 m
Cooking	1 h
Total Time	2 h 30 m

Nutritional Information:

Calories	245 kcal
Fat	3.2 g
Carbohydrates	44.1g
Protein	8.7 g
Cholesterol	73 mg
Sodium	420 mg

* Percent Daily Values are based on a 2,000 calorie diet.

Hungarian Sour Cream Bake

Ingredients

- 6 potatoes
- 8 eggs
- seasoning salt to taste
- 1 C. margarine
- 1 (16 oz.) container sour cream

Directions

- Set your oven to 350 degrees before doing anything else.
- Get your potatoes boiling in water and salt for 20 mins then remove all the liquids, peel, and slice the potatoes once they have cooled.
- Now get your eggs boiling in water for 1 min, place a lid on the pot, then shut the heat.
- Let the eggs stand for 12 mins in the water, then drain the liquid, peel the eggs, and slice them.
- Get a baking dish and lay your potato and eggs in it. Top each layer with some seasoned salt.
- Melt your sour cream and margarine in the pan then pour it over the contents in the baking dish.
- Add some more seasoned salt then cook everything in the oven for 35 mins. Enjoy.

Amount per serving (10 total)

Timing Information:

Preparation	45 m
Cooking	30 m
Total Time	1 h 15 m

Nutritional Information:

Calories	415 kcal
Fat	31.6 g
Carbohydrates	25.6g
Protein	8.8 g
Cholesterol	169 mg
Sodium	295 mg

* Percent Daily Values are based on a 2,000 calorie diet.

Hungarian Mashed Liver

Ingredients

- 2 tbsps vegetable oil
- 1 tbsp unsalted butter (optional)
- 1 large white onion, diced
- 2 lbs fresh chicken livers
- 6 hard-cooked eggs
- 1 small white onion, finely diced
- 1 bunch green onions, diced
- salt and pepper to taste
- 2 tbsps paprika
- 2 tbsps diced fresh parsley, divided
- 1 head romaine lettuce
- 2 sprigs fresh parsley

Directions

- Stir fry your onions in butter and oil until they are tender then add the livers and fry them with a high level of heat.
- Once the meat is fully done i.e. juices are clear, place everything in a bowl.
- Get a masher or large fork and mash the livers. Remove the membranes as you mash everything.
- Get 2nd bowl and beat your eggs in it then combine it with the mashed meat.

- Add in the green onions and the diced onions and combine everything evenly.
- Top everything with some pepper, salt, 1 tbsp parsley, and 1 tbsp of paprika.
- Stir the spices in then place everything in the fridge for 3 hrs.
- Layer your pieces of lettuce on a serving dish then garnish the lettuce with the liver and some more parsley and paprika.
- Enjoy.

Amount per serving (8 total)

Timing Information:

Preparation	10 m
Cooking	3 h 20 m
Total Time	3 h 30 m

Nutritional Information:

Calories	258 kcal
Fat	14.1 g
Carbohydrates	8.5g
Protein	24.4 g
Cholesterol	573 mg
Sodium	1116 mg

* Percent Daily Values are based on a 2,000 calorie diet.

BACON POTATOES AND CHICKEN

Ingredients

- 3 slices bacon
- 1 (3 lb) whole chicken, cut into pieces
- 1 tsp salt
- 1 tsp ground black pepper
- 2 onions, diced
- 1 tbsp paprika
- 1 tsp caraway seeds
- 4 potatoes, cut into large chunks
- 1/2 C. sour cream
- 1/4 C. diced fresh parsley
- 1 tbsp garlic powder

Directions

- Fry your bacon for 12 mins then place the bacon to the side and break everything into pieces.
- Keep about 2 tbsp of drippings in the pan and throw away the rest. Coat your chicken with some pepper and salt and fry the chicken in the bacon drippings for 12 mins with high heat.
- Now remove the chicken from the pan.
- Begin to stir fry your onions for 7 mins in the same pan, set the heat to low, and add in the caraway seeds and paprika.
- Stir the spices into the onions and add the chicken back in.

- Place a lid on the pot and let the chicken cook for 30 mins with a low level of heat.
- Now combine in the potatoes and place the lid back on the pot.
- Continue cooking the mix for 30 more mins then place everything in a serving dish.
- Add the garlic powder, parsley, and sour cream to the pan and stir the mix until it is smooth for 4 mins then top the chicken with it.
- Garnish everything with the bacon.
- Enjoy.

Amount per serving (4 total)

Timing Information:

Preparation	15 m
Cooking	1 h 30 m
Total Time	1 h 45 m

Nutritional Information:

Calories	23.7 g
Fat	52.4g
Carbohydrates	65.2 g
Protein	1190 mg
Cholesterol	938 mg
Sodium	23.7 g

* Percent Daily Values are based on a 2,000 calorie diet.

Hungarian Cream Cheese Cookies

Ingredients

- 1 lb butter, softened
- 1 lb cream cheese, softened
- 4 C. sifted all-purpose flour
- 1 lb walnuts, ground
- 1 C. white sugar
- 2 tbsps milk, or more as needed

Directions

- Get a bowl and with a stand mixer combine your cream and butter until it is frothy.
- Slowly mix in 2 C. of flour to form a dough.
- Now combine in the rest of the flour (2 C.) with your hands.
- Shape the dough into a ball then place everything into a bowl.
- Place a covering of plastic on the bowl and put everything in the fridge for 8 hrs.
- Now set your oven to 375 degrees before doing anything else.
- Get a bowl, combine: sugar and walnuts.
- Add the milk to the mix and stir everything until it is creamy.
- Knead your dough on a cutting board coated with flour, for 5 mins, then roll out the dough and cut it into two inch squares.

- Top each square with 1 tsp of walnut mix and place everything on a cookie sheet.
- Cook everything in the oven for 13 mins.
- Enjoy.

Amount per serving (36 total)

Timing Information:

Preparation	15 m
Cooking	10 m
Total Time	8 h 25 m

Nutritional Information:

Calories	289 kcal
Fat	23 g
Carbohydrates	18.3g
Protein	4.4 g
Cholesterol	41 mg
Sodium	111 mg

* Percent Daily Values are based on a 2,000 calorie diet.

Vegetable Hungarian Stew

Ingredients

- 3 tbsps olive oil
- 1 onion, diced
- 2 tbsps Hungarian sweet paprika
- 8 oz. textured vegetable protein
- 1 green bell pepper, diced
- 5 C. vegetable broth
- 4 large potatoes, diced

- 2 large carrots, diced
- 1 tomato, diced
- 1/2 tsp salt
- 1/2 tsp ground black pepper
- 2 tbsps diced fresh parsley
- 1 egg
- 1 C. all-purpose flour
- 1/2 tsp salt
- 2 tbsps water as needed

Directions

- Stir fry your onions in oil until they are soft then combine in: green peppers, veggie protein, and paprika. Stir the mix to coat the veggie protein with the spice.
- Now add in the parsley, broth, black pepper, potatoes, half tsp salt, carrots, and tomato.
- Get everything boiling, place a lid on the pot, set the heat to low, and let the mix gently boil until the potatoes are almost soft.

- Get a bowl, combine: 1/2 tsp salt, egg, and flour. Add some water just to make the mix smooth then place the dough on a plate.
- Drop tsp dollops of the mix into the soup as it cooks.
- Continue adding dumplings to the soup until all the dough has been combined in.
- Let the mix continue to gently boil until the veggies are soft.
- Enjoy.

Amount per serving (3 total)

Timing Information:

Preparation	10 m
Cooking	1 h
Total Time	1 h 10 m

Nutritional Information:

Calories	1014 kcal
Fat	20.5 g
Carbohydrates	140.1g
Protein	80.4 g
Cholesterol	162 mg
Sodium	2064 mg

* Percent Daily Values are based on a 2,000 calorie diet.

POTATO AND COCONUT DESSERT

Ingredients

- 1 1/4 C. mashed potatoes
- 1 1/4 C. confectioners' sugar
- 2 tbsps unsweetened cocoa powder
- 1/4 C. lemon juice
- 2 tbsps rum flavored extract
- 1/2 C. raisins
- 1 1/4 C. flaked coconut
- 1 tsp lemon zest
- 1/4 C. flaked coconut

Directions

- Get a bowl, submerge your raisins in lemon juice and rum.
- Get a 2nd bowl, combine: cocoa, mashed potatoes, and confectioners. Stir the mix then add in 1.25 C. of coconut and raisin mix.
- Shape everything into balls then place them all in the fridge for 2 days.
- Enjoy.

Amount per serving (24 total)

Timing Information:

Preparation	
Cooking	10 m
Total Time	10 m

Nutritional Information:

Calories	71 kcal
Fat	1.8 g
Carbohydrates	13.3g
Protein	0.6 g
Cholesterol	< 1 mg
Sodium	< 45 mg

* Percent Daily Values are based on a 2,000 calorie diet.

Maggie's Favorite Goulash

Ingredients

- 2 tbsps butter
- 2 large onions, diced
- 2 lbs flank steak
- 1/8 tsp caraway seed
- 1/4 tsp dried marjoram
- 1 clove garlic, minced
- 5 tbsps paprika
- 2 C. water
- 4 large potatoes, peeled and cubed
- salt and pepper to taste

Directions

- Stir fry your onions in butter with high heat until they are tender then begin to brown your beef all over.
- Add: the paprika, caraway, garlic, and marjoram.
- Stir the spices into the meat then submerge everything in water.
- Get the mix boiling, set the heat to low, and let the mix cook for 2.5 hrs.
- Now add the potatoes and continue simmering the mix for 50 more mins then add some pepper and salt.
- Enjoy.

Amount per serving (6 total)

Timing Information:

Preparation	20 m
Cooking	3 h 30 m
Total Time	3 h 50 m

Nutritional Information:

Calories	339 kcal
Fat	15.7 g
Carbohydrates	29.1g
Protein	21.8 g
Cholesterol	58 mg
Sodium	84 mg

* Percent Daily Values are based on a 2,000 calorie diet.

Honey Dessert

Ingredients

- 4 C. all-purpose flour
- 1 1/2 tsps baking soda
- 1 C. confectioners' sugar
- 1/3 C. unsalted butter
- 2 eggs, beaten
- 1/4 C. honey, warmed
- 1/4 C. sour cream
- 2 C. confectioners' sugar
- 3/4 C. vanilla sugar
- 1/4 C. all-purpose flour
- 1 C. milk
- 1 C. unsalted butter
- 1/4 C. confectioners' sugar for dusting

Directions

- Cover a cookie sheet with parchment paper then set your oven to 350 degrees before doing anything else.
- Get a bowl, combine: 1 C. confectioners, 4 C. of flour, and baking soda. Add in a third of a C. of butter with a pastry blender or with your hands, make a crumbly mix. Then add in the sour cream, honey, and eggs. Work the mix until it becomes a dough.
- Break the dough into 4 pieces then shape each into a rectangle.
- Lay everything on the cookie sheet and cook it in the oven for 17 mins.

- Now begin to heat and stir 1/4 C. flour, 2 C. confectioners, vanilla sugar, and sugar.
- Begin to stir the mix and slowly add in your milk.
- Continue heating and stirring the mix until it is thick. Then shut the heat add in the butter.
- Top one piece of pastry with one third of the sweet sauce, then lay another piece of pastry.
- Top this layer with more sauce and continue doing this until all the sauce has been used.
- Coat everything with confectioners.
- Enjoy.

Amount per serving (12 total)

Timing Information:

Preparation	30 m
Cooking	20 m
Total Time	1 h 20 m

Nutritional Information:

Calories	576 kcal
Fat	23.2 g
Carbohydrates	87.2g
Protein	6.7 g
Cholesterol	89 mg
Sodium	184 mg

* Percent Daily Values are based on a 2,000 calorie diet.

EASY HUNGARIAN GOULASH

Ingredients

- 1/4 C. vegetable oil
- 2 C. diced onion
- 3 green bell peppers, diced
- 3 tbsps tomato paste
- 1 lb lean top sirloin beef - cut into 1 inch cubes
- 1 pinch cayenne pepper
- 1 tsp paprika
- 2 cloves garlic, minced
- 1/2 tsp salt
- 6 C. beef broth
- 1 tbsp lemon juice
- 1/4 tsp caraway seeds
- 1 C. sour cream (optional)

Directions

- Stir fry your onions in veggie oil for 7 mins then stir in the tomato paste and green peppers.
- Place a lid on the pan, set the heat to low, and let the mix cook for 12 mins.
- Now add the beef to the pan along with: the lemon juice, cayenne, broth, paprika, caraway seeds, salt, and garlic.
- Let the mix gently boil for 90 mins.
- Once the mix has cooled off a bit add in your sour cream and stir everything. Enjoy.

Amount per serving (6 total)

Timing Information:

Preparation	25 m
Cooking	1 h 45 m
Total Time	2 h 15 m

Nutritional Information:

Calories	351 kcal
Fat	20.4 g
Carbohydrates	15.5g
Protein	27.1 g
Cholesterol	46 mg
Sodium	1590 mg

* Percent Daily Values are based on a 2,000 calorie diet.

BEEF AND PEPPER BAKE

Ingredients

- 9 yellow bell peppers
- 1/2 C. uncooked white rice
- 2 lbs lean ground beef
- 1 egg
- 1 onion, diced
- salt and pepper to taste
- 2 (12 fluid oz.) cans tomato juice
- 1/2 C. sour cream
- 1 tbsp all-purpose flour

Directions

- Slice off the top portion of the peppers then remove the insides.
- Get your rice boiling in water for 2 mins, then shut the heat and remove the liquid.
- Get a bowl, combine: pepper, rice, salt, beef, onion, and eggs.
- Evenly divide the beef mix between your peppers then place the stuffed peppers into a large pot. Add your tomato juice to the pot, place a lid on the pot and gently boil the peppers for 1.5 hrs, with a low level of heat.
- Get a 2nd bowl combine flour and sour cream.
- Add in 1 C. of the tomato mix then add it back to the pot.
- Continue gently boiling everything for 7 more mins.
- Enjoy.

Amount per serving (9 total)

Timing Information:

Preparation	30 m
Cooking	1 h 30 m
Total Time	2 h

Nutritional Information:

Calories	341 kcal
Fat	16.2 g
Carbohydrates	26.2g
Protein	23.7 g
Cholesterol	87 mg
Sodium	295 mg

* Percent Daily Values are based on a 2,000 calorie diet.

Sausage and Pepper Bake

Ingredients

- 1/3 C. ground Italian sausage
- 1 (8 oz.) package cream cheese, softened
- 3/4 tbsp garlic salt
- 3 tbsps grated Romano cheese
- 1 tsp dried oregano
- 1 tsp dried basil
- 1/3 C. Italian-style dry bread crumbs
- 1 tbsp olive oil
- 6 Hungarian hot peppers, cored and seeded

Directions

- Fry your sausage until fully done then break the meat into pieces.
- Now set your oven to 350 degrees before doing anything else.
- Get a bowl, combine: olive oil, sausage, bread crumbs, cream cheese, basil, garlic salt, oregano, and Romano.
- Fill your peppers with the mix and place everything on a cookie sheet and cook the peppers in the oven for 22 mins.
- Enjoy.

Amount per serving (6 total)

Timing Information:

Preparation	15 m
Cooking	20 m
Total Time	35 m

Nutritional Information:

Calories	243 kcal
Fat	20.6 g
Carbohydrates	8.1g
Protein	7 g
Cholesterol	54 mg
Sodium	1041 mg

* Percent Daily Values are based on a 2,000 calorie diet.

Hungarian Stew

Ingredients

- 3 tbsps olive oil
- 2 lbs green bell peppers, seeded and cubed
- 1 onion, diced
- 2 (14.5 oz.) cans diced tomatoes
- salt and pepper to taste
- 1/4 C. paprika
- 6 eggs
- 4 slices rye bread

Directions

- Stir fry your green pepper, and onions in olive oil for 12 mins then combine in the paprika, pepper, salt, and tomatoes.
- Continue frying the mix for 12 more mins.
- Get a bowl to beat your eggs in it.
- Make some space in your pan then add in the eggs in the new space.
- Let the eggs get slightly set then once they are almost done cooking, stir the mix, and cook everything 6 more mins.
- Enjoy with some toasted bread.

Amount per serving (4 total)

Timing Information:

Preparation	10 m
Cooking	30 m
Total Time	40 m

Nutritional Information:

Calories	415 kcal
Fat	21.6 g
Carbohydrates	40.7g
Protein	16 g
Cholesterol	208 mg
Sodium	649 mg

* Percent Daily Values are based on a 2,000 calorie diet.

HUNGARIAN BREAD SPICE

Maggie's Thoughts: Use this mix for any dough to give it a unique taste.

Ingredients

- 1/2 lb poppy seeds
- 1 C. milk
- 1/4 C. margarine
- 3/4 C. white sugar
- 1 pinch salt
- 2 eggs, beaten

Directions

- Get a mortar and pestle and mash your poppy seeds.
- With a low level of heat combine and stir the following: sugar, margarine, and milk.
- Stir the mix until it is smooth then combine half of it with the whisked eggs in a bowl and add the egg mix back into the pot.
- Keep heating the mix and stirring it until everything is thick then add in the poppy seeds.
- Enjoy.

Amount per serving (16 total)

Timing Information:

Preparation	10 m
Cooking	20 m
Total Time	1 h

Nutritional Information:

Calories	152 kcal
Fat	10 g
Carbohydrates	13.5g
Protein	3.8 g
Cholesterol	22 mg
Sodium	50 mg

* Percent Daily Values are based on a 2,000 calorie diet.

Mustard and Paprika Chicken

Ingredients

- 4 skinless, boneless chicken breast halves - flattened to 1/2 inch thickness
- 3 eggs
- 2 tbsps Hungarian paprika, divided
- 2 tbsps prepared yellow mustard
- salt and pepper to taste
- 2 C. matzo meal
- 1 C. oil for frying

Directions

- Get a bowl, combine: pepper, eggs, salt, 1 tbsp of paprika, and mustard.
- Get a 2nd bowl combine: matzo meal and paprika.
- Coat your chicken first with eggs then with the dry mix and fry the pieces of chicken in hot oil for 6 mins.
- Flip the chicken and continue frying everything for 6 more mins.
- Enjoy.

Amount per serving (4 total)

Timing Information:

Preparation	20 m
Cooking	20 m
Total Time	40 m

Nutritional Information:

Calories	468 kcal
Fat	12.9 g
Carbohydrates	54.7g
Protein	35.6 g
Cholesterol	207 mg
Sodium	203 mg

* Percent Daily Values are based on a 2,000 calorie diet.

Hungarian Chicken

Ingredients

- 3 eggs, beaten
- 1/2 C. water
- 2 1/2 C. all-purpose flour
- 2 tsps salt
- 1/4 C. butter
- 1 1/2 lbs bone-in chicken pieces, with skin
- 1 medium onion, diced
- 1 1/2 C. water
- 1 tbsp paprika
- 1/2 tsp salt
- 1 tsp ground black pepper
- 2 tbsps all-purpose flour
- 1 C. sour cream

Directions

- Get a saucepan of water boiling.
- Get a bowl, combine: half C. water, eggs, and 2 tsp of salt. Then slowly add in 2.5 C. of flour.
- Drop dollops of the mix into the boiling water and cook it for 12 mins until they begin to float then place the dumplings in a colander.
- Cook 3 to 4 dumplings at a time.
- Begin to brown your chicken, in butter, in a frying pan, on both sides then add in the onions and continue frying everything for 7 more mins.
- Add in 1.5 C. of water: pepper, salt, and paprika.

- Stir the mix then let everything continue to fry for 12 mins.
- Once the chicken is fully done remove the chicken from the pan.
- Add in the sour cream and 2 tbsps of flour to the onions.
- Stir the heat the mix until it is simmering.
- Continue simmering the mix until everything is thick then add your dumplings to the sour cream mix and serve it with the chicken.
- Enjoy.

Amount per serving (4 total)

Timing Information:

Preparation	30 m
Cooking	30 m
Total Time	1 h

Nutritional Information:

Calories	961 kcal
Fat	54 g
Carbohydrates	69.2g
Protein	47.4 g
Cholesterol	323 mg
Sodium	11745 mg

* Percent Daily Values are based on a 2,000 calorie diet.

VINEGAR SALAD

Ingredients

- 2 large seedless English cucumbers, sliced thin
- 1 extra large onions, sliced thin
- 1/4 C. diced fresh dill
- 3 tbsps white vinegar
- 3 tbsps vegetable oil
- 1 tsp salt, or to taste
- 1/2 tsp ground black pepper, or to taste

Directions

- Get a bowl combine: dill, onions, and cucumbers.
- Add in the vinegar and stir everything. Then add in the oil, some pepper, some salt, and stir the mix again.
- Enjoy.

Amount per serving (6 total)

Timing Information:

Preparation	
Cooking	15 m
Total Time	15 m

Nutritional Information:

Calories	98 kcal
Fat	7 g
Carbohydrates	8.9g
Protein	1.3 g
Cholesterol	0 mg
Sodium	393 mg

* Percent Daily Values are based on a 2,000 calorie diet.

PAPRIKA FISH

Ingredients

- 1 whole trout, cleaned
- 2 tsps lemon juice
- 1 tsp vegetable oil
- 1 tsp ground cumin
- 1 tsp chili powder
- 1 tsp spicy Hungarian paprika
- 1/4 tsp ground black pepper
- 1 pinch salt
- cooking spray

Directions

- Cut some incisions into your fish on all sides.
- Get a bowl, combine: salt, lemon juice, black pepper, veggie oil, paprika, cumin, and chili powder.
- Stir the mix into a topping then coat your fish with it.
- Place the fish on a platter and place a covering of plastic around everything.
- Put the fish in the fridge for 60 mins.
- Now get your outdoor grill hot then coat the grate with oil.
- Wrap the fish in some foil and place it on the grill for 6 mins each side.
- Enjoy.

Amount per serving (2 total)

Timing Information:

Preparation	10 m
Cooking	10 m
Total Time	1 h 20 m

Nutritional Information:

Calories	234 kcal
Fat	10.8 g
Carbohydrates	2.5g
Protein	< 31.1 g
Cholesterol	92 mg
Sodium	284 mg

* Percent Daily Values are based on a 2,000 calorie diet.

CZECH PANCAKES

Ingredients

- 4 large potatoes
- 3 cloves garlic, crushed
- salt and black pepper to taste
- 1 pinch dried marjoram (optional)
- 2 tsps caraway seeds (optional)
- 2 eggs
- 1 tbsp milk
- 3 tbsps all-purpose flour
- oil for frying

Directions

- Remove the skins from your potatoes and grate them.
- Place everything in a bowl with: the caraway seeds, crushed garlic, marjoram, salt, and pepper.
- Combine your milk and eggs until they are smooth then pour the mix into the potatoes.
- Slowly add in your flour to make a batter.
- Get a quarter of an inch of olive oil hot then being to fry 1.4 C. of batter for 4 mins each side. Continue frying the potato pancakes in this manner.
- Enjoy.

Amount per serving (3 total)

Timing Information:

Preparation	30 m
Cooking	30 m
Total Time	1 h

Nutritional Information:

Calories	527 kcal
Fat	11.1 g
Carbohydrates	94.3g
Protein	15.1 g
Cholesterol	110 mg
Sodium	74 mg

* Percent Daily Values are based on a 2,000 calorie diet.

All Pork and Sausage Stew

Ingredients

- 1 lb dry garbanzo beans, soaked for 8 hrs in water
- 1 pig's tail, cut into 1 inch pieces
- 2 pig's ears, diced
- 1 lb chorizo, sliced into chunks
- 1/2 lb pork shoulder, cubed
- 6 oz. pancetta bacon, diced
- 1 onion, diced
- 3 carrots, coarsely diced
- 4 stalks celery, diced
- 6 cloves garlic, diced
- 1 red bell pepper, diced
- 1 1/2 tsps Hungarian sweet paprika
- salt and pepper to taste

Directions

- Add the following to a large pot: pig's tail, ears, and shoulder, garlic, chorizo, bell pepper, pancetta, celery, carrots, some pepper, some salt, paprika, garbanzos, and onions.
- Submerge everything in water and get it all boiling.
- Once the mix is boiling place a lid on the pot, set the heat to a low to medium level, and let the mix gently cook for 90 mins.
- As everything cooks remove the fat that rises to the top.
- Enjoy.

Amount per serving (8 total)

Timing Information:

Preparation	45 m
Cooking	2 h
Total Time	10 h 45 m

Nutritional Information:

Calories	779 kcal
Fat	49.5 g
Carbohydrates	41.7g
Protein	41.5 g
Cholesterol	121 mg
Sodium	1005 mg

* Percent Daily Values are based on a 2,000 calorie diet.

Hungary Pepper Salsa

Ingredients

- 2 medium heirloom tomatoes
- 1 C. fresh or frozen wild blueberries
- 3/4 C. diced sweet onion
- 2 cloves garlic, minced
- 2 tbsps rice vinegar
- 2 tbsps olive oil
- 1 jalapeno pepper, finely diced
- 1/2 Hungarian hot pepper, finely diced
- 2 tbsps diced fresh cilantro
- 2 tbsps diced Italian flat leaf parsley
- salt and pepper to taste

Directions

- Cut a few incisions into your tomatoes and boil them in water for 1 min. Then place them in a bowl of cold water. Now remove the skins, cut them in half, and throw away the seeds. Dice the tomatoes and place them in a bowl with: parsley, blue berries, cilantro, onions, Hungarian pepper, jalapenos, and garlic. Stir the mix then add in the olive oil and rice vinegar. Then stir everything again.
- Add in some pepper and salt and place a covering of plastic on the bowl. Put everything in the fridge for 8 hrs. Enjoy.

Amount per serving (8 total)

Timing Information:

Preparation	
Cooking	30 m
Total Time	8 h 30 m

Nutritional Information:

Calories	55 kcal
Fat	3.5 g
Carbohydrates	5.8g
Protein	0.7 g
Cholesterol	0 mg
Sodium	3 mg

* Percent Daily Values are based on a 2,000 calorie diet.

Hungarian Dump Dinner

Ingredients

- 2 lbs ground pork
- 2 vine-ripened tomatoes, diced small
- 1 yellow bell peppers, diced
- 1 (20 oz.) can pineapple chunks, drained
- 1 (15.5 oz.) can black beans, drained
- 1 (11 oz.) can whole kernel corn, drained
- 1 (12 oz.) can tomato paste
- 3/4 C. diced green onions
- 1 C. diced baby corn
- 1 1/4 C. hard apple cider
- 4 cloves garlic, minced
- 2 tbsps brown sugar
- 2 tsps salt
- 1 tbsp Hungarian sweet paprika
- 1 tsp ground black pepper
- 1 tbsp molasses
- 1/4 tsp ground ancho chile pepper
- 1/4 tsp dried sage
- 3/4 tsp curry powder
- 1 pinch ground cinnamon
- 1 1/2 tsps honey
- 1 tbsp white vinegar

Directions

- Fry your pork until it is fully done then remove all the oils.

- Now add the following to the crock pot of a slow cooker: vinegar, pork, honey, tomato, cinnamon, bell peppers, curry powder, pineapple, sage, beans, ancho pepper, kernel corn, molasses, tomato paste, pepper, onions, paprika, salt, baby corn, brown sugar, cider, and garlic.
- Stir the mix a bit until it is evenly combined then place the lid on the slow cooker.
- Cook everything for 5 hrs with a high level of heat.
- Enjoy.

Amount per serving (10 total)

Timing Information:

Preparation	30 m
Cooking	5 h 10 m
Total Time	5 h 40 m

Nutritional Information:

Calories	422 kcal
Fat	20.1 g
Carbohydrates	39.8g
Protein	21.3 g
Cholesterol	65 mg
Sodium	1056 mg

* Percent Daily Values are based on a 2,000 calorie diet.

Dumplings from Hungary

Ingredients

- 2 eggs
- 1/2 tsp salt
- 3/4 C. water
- 2 C. all-purpose flour
- 1 large pot filled with salted boiling water
- 1 C. melted butter

Directions

- Get a pot of water and salt boiling.
- Now get a bowl, combine: water, salt, eggs.
- Beat the mix until it is smooth then slowly add in your flour.
- Work the mix until it becomes a dough then leave it for 12 mins.
- Begin to knead the mix a bit for 2 more mins then drop tsp sized dollops in the boiling water.
- Submerge the spoon in the water to get the dough to fall off easier.
- Cook 4 dumplings at a time until they begin to float then place them in a bowl.
- Once everything has been cooked add the dumplings to a skillet and sear them in some melted butter.
- Enjoy.

Amount per serving: 4

Timing Information:

Preparation	10 mins
Total Time	15 mins

Nutritional Information:

Calories	263.2
Fat	2.9g
Cholesterol	93.0mg
Sodium	328.7mg
Carbohydrates	47.8g
Protein	9.6g

* Percent Daily Values are based on a 2,000 calorie diet.

EASTERN EUROPEAN BREAKFAST

Ingredients

- 5 tbsps butter
- 1 medium onion, diced
- 1 C. mushroom, sliced
- 6 eggs, beaten
- 1/2 tsp salt
- 1/2 tsp black pepper
- 1/2 tsp sweet paprika, Hungarian

Directions

- Stir fry your onions in butter for 12 mins then add in the paprika and mushrooms.
- Let the veggies cook for 7 mins then set the heat to low.
- Get a bowl, combine: black pepper, salt, and eggs.
- Pour this mix into the pan with the eggs then cook everything for 12 mins.
- Get a spatula and lift a section of the eggs and let the uncooked eggs run underneath.
- Continue cooking the omelet in this manner until it done.
- Top the omelet with some green onions and sour cream.
- Enjoy.

Amount per serving: 4

Timing Information:

| Preparation | 20 mins |
| Total Time | 20 mins |

Nutritional Information:

Calories	250.9
Fat	21.6g
Cholesterol	317.1mg
Sodium	526.1mg
Carbohydrates	4.0g
Protein	10.4g

* Percent Daily Values are based on a 2,000 calorie diet.

RUSTIC ROAST

Ingredients

- 3 lbs chuck roast or 3 lbs rump roast
- 1 tbsp paprika
- 2 tsps salt
- 1/4 tsp pepper
- 2 tbsps vegetable oil
- 1/2 C. water
- 1 bay leaf
- 1 (4 oz.) cans sliced mushrooms, drained
- 8 -10 onions, small white
- 8 small carrots, cut or whole
- 2 tbsps parsley, minced
- 2 (8 oz.) cans tomato sauce
- 1 C. sour cream
- cooked small noodles or boiled potatoes

Directions

- Coat your meat with pepper, salt, and paprika then brown it on all sides in a saucepan.
- Add the bay leaf and also the water.
- Place a lid on the pot and let the mix cook for 90 mins.
- Add in the carrots, onions and mushrooms around the meat and then add in the tomato sauce.

- Place the lid back on the pot and continue cooking everything for 1 hr with a low level of heat.
- Now stir in the parsley and also the sour cream.
- Enjoy.

Amount per serving: 6

Timing Information:

Preparation	15 mins
Total Time	3 hrs 15 mins

Nutritional Information:

Calories	543.9
Fat	26.5g
Cholesterol	169.6mg
Sodium	1443.6mg
Carbohydrates	27.3g
Protein	52.7g

* Percent Daily Values are based on a 2,000 calorie diet.

TOMATO RIBS

Ingredients

- 4 lbs short rib of beef
- 2 tbsps cooking oil
- 2 medium onions, sliced
- 1 (15 oz.) tomato sauce
- 1 C. water
- 1/4 C. brown sugar
- 1/4 C. vinegar
- 1 tsp salt
- 1 tsp dry mustard
- 1 tbsp Worcestershire sauce
- 4 1/2 C. medium noodles
- 1 C. water

Directions

- Brown your ribs, in a saucepan, in oil. Place the ribs to the side and begin to stir fry your onions until tender. Now add the ribs back in.
- Get a bowl, combine: Worcestershire, tomato sauce, mustard, 1 C. water, salt, brown sugar, and vinegar.
- Stir the mix until it is smooth then top your ribs with it.
- Get everything boiling then once it is, set the heat to low, and let the mix gently simmer for 2.5 hrs.
- Now remove any fats then add in 1 more C. of water and the noodles.
- Place a lid on the pot and let the mix gently boil for 17 more mins.
- Enjoy.

Amount per serving: 6

Timing Information:

Preparation	20 mins
Total Time	2 hrs 20 mins

Nutritional Information:

Calories	1451.3
Fat	116.8g
Cholesterol	264.6mg
Sodium	950.4mg
Carbohydrates	47.1g
Protein	50.4g

* Percent Daily Values are based on a 2,000 calorie diet.

HUNGARIAN TOPPING FOR BREAD

Ingredients

- 8 oz. cream cheese
- 1 C. cottage cheese
- 3 tbsps capers
- 1 tsp caraway seed
- 1/2 tsp dry mustard
- 2 tsps paprika

Directions

- Get a bowl, combine the following until it is creamy: paprika, cream cheese, dry mustard, cottage cheese, caraway seeds, and capers.
- Place a covering of plastic on the bowl and put everything in the fridge for 8 hrs.
- Serve the mix on some toasted rye bread.
- Enjoy.

Amount per serving: 12

Timing Information:

| Preparation | 10 mins |
| Total Time | 10 mins |

Nutritional Information:

Calories	86.7
Fat	7.5g
Cholesterol	23.4mg
Sodium	190.7mg
Carbohydrates	1.4g
Protein	3.7g

* Percent Daily Values are based on a 2,000 calorie diet.

POTATOES FROM EASTERN EUROPE

Ingredients

- 6 medium potatoes, cooked and sliced
- 1/2 C. melted butter or 1/2 C. margarine
- 4 large hard-boiled eggs, diced
- 2 C. sour cream, about 16 oz
- 1 1/2 tsps salt
- 1/4 tsp pepper
- 1 C. fine dry breadcrumb
- 1/2 C. green onion, diced
- paprika

Directions

- Set your oven to 350 degrees before doing anything else.
- Get a bowl, combine: pepper, eggs, salt, and sour cream.
- Add your melted butter to a baking dish then layer half of the following over it: sour cream mix, potatoes, bread crumbs, and green onions.
- Layer everything again then top it all with the paprika.
- Cook everything in the oven for 35 mins.
- Enjoy.

Amount per serving: 12

Timing Information:

Preparation	10 mins
Total Time	40 mins

Nutritional Information:

Calories	884.0
Fat	54.1g
Cholesterol	323.6mg
Sodium	1377.3mg
Carbohydrates	81.7g
Protein	20.4g

* Percent Daily Values are based on a 2,000 calorie diet.

MUSHROOMS AND SOUR CREAM STEW

Ingredients

- 3 slices bacon, diced, turkey
- 3 tbsps butter
- 1/2 C. sliced mushrooms
- 1/2 C. diced onion
- 2 lbs veal, cut in cubes
- 1/2 C. chicken broth
- 1 C. sour cream
- 1 tsp salt
- 1/2 tsp black pepper
- 1 tsp paprika

Directions

- Set your oven to 250 degrees before doing anything else.
- Begin to stir fry the following in butter: mushroom, bacon, and onions. Fry the mix until the bacon is done.
- Now place the mix in a casserole dish and then begin to brown your veal in the bacon drippings.
- Once the veal is browned all over place it in the casserole dish as well.
- Pour in the broth to the pan and also add in: sour cream, salt, paprika, and pepper.
- Get the mix boiling then add it to the casserole dish as well.
- Place a covering of foil over everything and cook it all in the oven for 65 mins. Enjoy.

Amount per serving: 4

Timing Information:

Preparation	20 mins
Total Time	1 hr 20 mins

Nutritional Information:

Calories	558.5
Fat	19.3g
Cholesterol	242.8mg
Sodium	1034.3mg
Carbohydrates	4.4g
Protein	47.0g

* Percent Daily Values are based on a 2,000 calorie diet.

CLASSICAL HUNGARIAN STEW (LECSÓ)

Ingredients

- 1 large onion, diced
- 3 tbsps olive oil
- 7 green bell peppers
- 3 large peeled tomatoes, diced
- 3 cloves garlic, diced
- 1/2 tsp chili
- 1 chorizo sausage, sliced into thin rings

Directions

- For 4 mins stir fry your garlic and onions in olive oil.
- Then add in the chili and sausage and continue frying everything for 7 mins.
- Now combine in the bell peppers, black pepper, and salt.
- Set the heat to low then stir in the tomatoes.
- Continue gently boiling the mix until you find that the peppers are soft.
- Enjoy

Amount per serving: 4

Timing Information:

Preparation	25 mins
Total Time	1 hr 10 mins

Nutritional Information:

Calories	258.8 kcal
Fat	16.7g
Cholesterol	13.3mg
Sodium	206.2mg
Carbohydrates	23.2g
Protein	7.8g

* Percent Daily Values are based on a 2,000 calorie diet.

PORK WITH CREAMY MUSHROOMS (JAGERSCHNITZEL)

Ingredients

- 1 C. bread crumbs
- 1 tbsp all-purpose flour
- salt and pepper to taste
- 2 tbsps vegetable oil
- 4 pork steaks or cutlets, flattened thin
- 1 egg, beaten
- 1 medium onion, diced
- 1 (8 oz.) can sliced mushrooms
- 1 1/2 C. water
- 1 cube beef bouillon
- 1 tbsp cornstarch
- 1/2 C. sour cream

Directions

- Get a bowl, combine: flour and bread crumbs.
- Get a 2nd bowl for your eggs.
- Coat your pieces of pork first with the eggs then with the dry mix.
- Begin to fry your pork for 6 mins each side then remove them from the pan.

- Add the mushrooms and onions to the pan and begin to fry them until the onions become see through and the mushrooms begin to sweat. Now add the water and the beef cube.
- Stir the mix until the cube fully dissolves in the water. Then let the mix simmer for 22 mins.
- Combine your sour cream and cornstarch together then add it to the simmering mushroom sauce.
- Stir the mix and let the contents continue to simmer over low heat for 2 more mins.
- Liberally top your pork with the mushroom sauce.
- Enjoy.

Amount per serving (4 total)

Timing Information:

Preparation	15 m
Cooking	25 m
Total Time	40 m

Nutritional Information:

Calories	556 kcal
Fat	33.5 g
Carbohydrates	29.9g
Protein	32.9 g
Cholesterol	157 mg
Sodium	683 mg

* Percent Daily Values are based on a 2,000 calorie diet.

DUMPLINGS IN GERMANY I (SPAETZLE)

Ingredients

- 1 C. all-purpose flour
- 1/4 C. milk
- 2 eggs
- 1/2 tsp ground nutmeg
- 1 pinch freshly ground white pepper
- 1/2 tsp salt
- 1 gallon hot water
- 2 tbsps butter
- 2 tbsps chopped fresh parsley

Directions

- Get a bowl, combine: nutmeg, whisked eggs, flour, milk, white pepper, and salt.
- Form a dough from this mix.
- Now press the dough through a cheese grater or through a sieve with large holes.
- Cook the dumplings in hot oil for 9 mins.
- Then place them on some paper towel.
- Continue frying in batches until everything has been cooked.
- Now take all your German dumplings and stir fry them in butter before topping with parsley. Enjoy.

Amount per serving (6 total)

Timing Information:

Preparation	10 m
Cooking	1 h
Total Time	1 h 10 m

Nutritional Information:

Calories	141 kcal
Fat	6 g
Carbohydrates	16.8g
Protein	4.7 g
Cholesterol	73 mg
Sodium	269 mg

* Percent Daily Values are based on a 2,000 calorie diet.

DUMPLINGS IN GERMANY II (SEMMELKNOEDEL)

Ingredients

- 1 (1 lb) loaf stale French bread, cut into 1 inch cubes
- 1 C. milk
- 2 tbsps butter
- 1 onion, finely chopped
- 1 tbsp chopped fresh parsley
- 2 eggs
- 1/2 tsp salt
- 1 pinch ground black pepper
- 1/2 C. dry bread crumbs (optional)

Directions

- Get your milk simmering in a pot.
- Get a bowl, combine: hot milk and bread.
- Let the bread stand for 17 mins.
- At the same time, stir fry your onions in butter, until soft, then add the parsley, and cook the mix for 2 more mins.

- Add this to the bread and also add: pepper, salt, and beaten eggs.
- Now, using your hands, form the bread into a dough.
- Get 5 inches of water and salt boiling.
- Form a golf ball sized dumpling and place it in the boiling water.
- If the dumpling breaks apart while boiling add more bread to the dough and mix it all again.
- Otherwise divide your dough into golf ball sized dumplings and cook everything in the water for 22 mins.
- Enjoy.

Amount per serving (4 total)

Timing Information:

Preparation	30 m
Cooking	20 m
Total Time	50 m

Nutritional Information:

Calories	506 kcal
Fat	12.3 g
Carbohydrates	78.8g
Protein	20.5 g
Cholesterol	113 mg
Sodium	1220 mg

* Percent Daily Values are based on a 2,000 calorie diet.

Cabbage and Apples

Ingredients

- 2 tbsps butter
- 5 C. shredded red cabbage
- 1 C. sliced green apples
- 1/3 C. apple cider vinegar
- 3 tbsps water
- 1/4 C. white sugar
- 2 1/4 tsps salt
- 1/4 tsp black pepper
- 1/4 tsp ground cloves

Directions

- Get the following boiling: pepper, butter, salt, cabbage, water, apples, cloves, vinegar, and sugar.
- Once the mix is boiling, place a lid on the pot, set the heat to a low level, and let everything cook for 2 hours with a gentle simmer.
- Enjoy.

Amount per serving (4 total)

Timing Information:

Preparation	20 m
Cooking	1 h 30 m
Total Time	1 h 50 m

Nutritional Information:

Calories	148 kcal
Fat	6 g
Carbohydrates	23.6g
Protein	1.4 g
Cholesterol	15 mg
Sodium	1375 mg

* Percent Daily Values are based on a 2,000 calorie diet.

Beef Rolls of Bacon, Onions, and Pickles (Rouladen)

Ingredients

- 1 1/2 lbs flank steak, 1/4 inch filets, 3 inches in width
- German stone ground mustard, to taste
- 1/2 lb thick sliced bacon
- 2 large onions, sliced
- 1 (16 oz.) jar dill pickle slices
- 2 tbsps butter
- 2 1/2 C. water
- 1 cube beef bouillon

Directions

- Top each piece of steak with mustard then layer: onions, pickles, and bacon on each.
- Shape the filet into a roll then place a toothpick in each to preserve the structure.
- Brown your steaks in butter then add in 2.5 C. of water and bouillon.
- Mix the bouillon and water together and then gently boil the rolls for 60 mins with a low level of heat.
- Enjoy.

Amount per serving (6 total)

Timing Information:

Preparation	20 m
Cooking	1 h 10 m
Total Time	1 h 30 m

Nutritional Information:

Calories	264 kcal
Fat	17.4 g
Carbohydrates	7.7g
Protein	19.1 g
Cholesterol	59 mg
Sodium	1450 mg

* Percent Daily Values are based on a 2,000 calorie diet.

EASTERN EUROPEAN MEAT PASTRIES

Ingredients

- 1/2 C. chopped onion
- 1 1/2 lbs lean ground beef
- 1 (16 oz.) can sauerkraut, drained and pressed dry
- 2 (8 oz.) cans refrigerated crescent rolls
- 1 (8 oz.) package shredded Cheddar cheese

Directions

- Set your oven to 350 degrees before doing anything else.
- Stir fry your beef and onions until the beef is fully done then remove all the excess oils before adding in your sauerkraut.
- Get everything hot and then shut the heat.
- Flatten your rolls and then place them into a casserole dish.
- Top the rolls with the onion mix and then layer the 2nd piece of dough on top.
- Crimp the edges of the two layers of dough together then top everything with some cheese.
- Cook the dish in the oven for 27 mins.
- Enjoy.

Amount per serving (6 total)

Timing Information:

Preparation	20 m
Cooking	25 m
Total Time	45 m

Nutritional Information:

Calories	674 kcal
Fat	42.3 g
Carbohydrates	32.5g
Protein	37.1 g
Cholesterol	114 mg
Sodium	894 mg

* Percent Daily Values are based on a 2,000 calorie diet.

THANKS FOR READING! NOW LET'S TRY SOME **SUSHI** AND **DUMP DINNERS**....

Send the Book!

To grab this **box set** simply follow the link mentioned above, or tap the book cover.

This will take you to a page where you can simply enter your email address and a PDF version of the **box set** will be emailed to you.

I hope you are ready for some serious cooking!

Send the Book!

You will also receive updates about all my new books when they are free.

Also don't forget to like and subscribe on the social networks. I love meeting my readers. Links to all my profiles are below so please click and connect :)

Facebook

Twitter

COME ON...
LET'S BE FRIENDS :)

I adore my readers and love connecting with them socially. Please follow the links below so we can connect on Facebook, Twitter, and Google+.

Facebook

Twitter

I also have a blog that I regularly update for my readers so check it out below.

My Blog

CAN I ASK A FAVOUR?

If you found this book interesting, or have otherwise found any benefit in it. Then may I ask that you post a review of it on Amazon? Nothing excites me more than new reviews, especially reviews which suggest new topics for writing. I do read all reviews and I always factor feedback into my newer works.

So if you are willing to take ten minutes to write what you sincerely thought about this book then please visit our Amazon page and post your opinions.

Again thank you!

Interested in Other Easy Cookbooks?

Everything is easy! Check out my Amazon Author page for more great cookbooks:

For a complete listing of all my books please see my author page.

Made in the USA
Lexington, KY
17 December 2016